# 7 Steps to Greatness Workbook



## The Workbook to Take Your Life, Studies, Career and Business to the Next Level

### Dr Patrick Businge

*Bestselling Author of 7 Steps to Greatness*

Published by Greatness University Publishers

www.greatness-university.com

ISBN 978-1-9999494-3-3

ISBN 1999949439

# DEDICATION

This workbook is dedicated to you.  You have something special. There is greatness within you. May the 7 steps help you unleash the greatness in you.

# CONTENTS

# ACKNOWLEDGEMENTS

This workbook would have not been possible without the mentoring of Les Brown: world's number one motivational speaker, Ona Brown: expert in personal transformation, Brian Tracy: bestselling author and world's top success coach, and Omar Periu: world leading wealth coach. I was also fortunate to come to the attention of Antonio Smith Jr, Founder of Plant Better University who wrote the foreword of my bestselling book *7 Steps to Greatness* on which this workbook is based.

I am indebted to colleagues in the Les Brown Maximum Achievement Team, Brian Tracy's Mastermind Group, and to Greatness University Maximum Achievement Team. It is because of their critical friendship and moral support that I have accomplished writing this workbook.

Special thanks to my family, relatives and friends. While my father Mr George Rusoke inspired my head, my mother Mrs Stella Rusoke ignited my heart. I cannot fail to thank my wife Mrs Julian Businge and my two little children for the patience and courtesy I received whilst writing this book. I cannot end without mentioning all my students and the great people from all over the world who have inspired me as I wrote this and other books.

# PREFACE

I first met Dr Patrick Businge at an event in Florida. Les Brown, the world's number 1 motivational speaker and our mentor, headlined the event. When I shared the stage with Patrick and listened to his message, I instantly knew there was something very special about him. Obviously, my gut feeling was correct. As if he was reading my mind, he introduced himself to me and I was introduced to the man behind the talent.

A few months later, the calm and mild-mannered man with a sweet accent asked me to write a foreword to his book *7 Steps to Greatness*. I agreed immediately. How could I resist honouring such an honourable figure after seeing people fall in love with his message in Florida? Patrick is a wonderful person who has managed to write one of the most practical books on self-help I have read in a long time. Follow his message and your life will be transformed.

Dr Patrick Businge's mind is saturated with universal truth. As you will discover in each step, he is passionate, sometimes to a fault, about being effective for greatness. I doubt if there is a person on the planet who knows both universal laws on greatness as well as practical application in depth as Dr Patrick Businge. This combination is at times mind-boggling.

Dr Patrick Businge is both the messenger and message of greatness in his books. From many interactions with him as a teacher, colleague and friend, my judgment is this: Dr Patrick Businge is a prosperous mind that keeps pace with the best. Almost without fail, a conversation with him will fill you with knowledge that surpasses all understanding. So, I am happy to entice all kinds of people to follow his pathway to greatness.

We all need a path to greatness and Dr Patrick Businge has provided one of the very best. May life be kind to all who read the *7 Steps to Greatness* and all its accompanying products for the wings of prosperity are tucked within, and they have no respect of person. If you want to fly, your wings and passport to any destination you desire will be found within his books. I love you all.

Antonio T. Smith, Jr, Bestselling author of *Keep Walking*

# CALLED TO GREATNESS

'Though no one can go back and make a brand new start, anyone can start from now and make a brand new ending'.
**Attributed to Carl Bard**

This is an exciting time to be alive. Our world is going through a lot of scientific breakthroughs and technological transformations. More than ever, we can connect and communicate with each other at a very faster rate using social media. We can now move easily from one continent to another for journeys that used to take months now take hours.  The question is: is your life moving to surpass this pace? The question is not will your life move- the question is where will your life move to?

In this workbook, you will discover the steps to take your life where from where it is to where you want it to go. You might be asking:  Can I really change my life in just 7 steps?  Let me answer your question. As you travel through the streets of life, you might have experienced moments such as falling in or out love, a car accident, burglary, medical diagnosis, passing an interview, bereavement, and many others. As you have gone through these moments your life might have changed in just a couple of seconds and it has never been the same again.

For some of us, the numerous activities in this workbook might be too much. Our lives might be changed by completing activities in a couple of steps. For others, going through all the activities in this workbook might be necessary so that they move closer to their greatness on a daily basis. As they move from activity to activity, the changes that they make might seem small but, with time, they will realise how far they have changed. Remember, as you step into your greatness, the changes that matter most are the changes that happen within you and not those that happen outside of you.  So, this workbook will help you go from where you are towards the greatness that awaits you.

# Choosing greatness

The world's number one motivational speaker Les Brown says, **'Greatness is a choice not a destiny'**. Like most people, you may not be aware that you have to choose to be great. Given that most people do not ask life changing questions, given that most people do not choose to be great, they die without manifesting their greatness. They leave this planet with their greatness unused.

This workbook is written for people who have the courage to follow their heart and step into their greatness. It is a designed for those who want to take the road less travelled and live fulfilled lives.  It is inspired by what I have experienced as I travelled to various parts of the world and lived among various great people.  It is informed by what I have learnt from my mother who lived in poverty but did not allow poverty to live in her. It is informed by what I have learnt from my father who was imprisoned because of his dream to educate me.  So, the 7 steps in this workbook are not hypothetical but are based the personal journey I have taken from a being missionary to a parent, from a student to teacher, from an author to an international speaker, from a migrant worker to a successful entrepreneur in the United Kingdom.

The content of this workbook is also based on the many years of research and unrivalled mentoring I have received. My mentors and other great people have helped millions of people live their dreams and not their fears. I have condensed all that I have learnt from them in this and other books. I am sharing with you this message because I believe in your dreams. I believe in your potential to take your life, business, studies, career to the next level and live a great life. Now is the time to step into your greatness.

It is often said that the first step is the hardest. In the first step to greatness, you are going to complete activities on searching and finding yourself. Who are you? What is at the core of your being? What makes you 'you'? Where have you been with your life? Once you have found yourself, you are given a special gift that contains your greatness. With this gift, your life is to take on a new meaning and your eyes are to open to see a new horizon. But you are not stopping here. You are going to take the next step.

In the second step to greatness, I am inviting you to compete activities centred on discovering your purpose in this immense universe. I am challenging you to answer the following questions: Why are you alive today? What has brought you to this planet? What is your burning desire? What is your personal mission? How are the future generations to know that your life was worth living? What is the vision for your life? What inspires you to get into action, be in action, and stay in action? Once you discover your purpose, you are to guard it like the apple of your eye. But you are not stopping here. You are climbing to the next step.

In the third step to greatness, you are going to complete activities that will allow you to dream big. You will dream big because you probably know from the author of *As a Man Thinketh*, James Allen, that **'dreamers are the saviours of the world'**. The big dreams you have will push you out of your comfort zone and you will witness defining moments unfold in your life. With this zeal and motivation, you will not stop here. You will crave to climb the next step.

Benjamin E Mays, American civil rights activist and spiritual mentor to Martin Luther King Jr, says, **'The tragedy of life doesn't lie in not reaching your goal. The tragedy lies in having no goal to reach'.** So, in the fourth step to greatness, you are going to set S.T.A.R© goals. You are invited to have goals that are strongly felt in your heart and are connected to your dreams. You are able to visualise these goals in the theatre of your mind. Your goals are to be absolutely necessary that they become a life and death issue to you. Your goals are difficult to achieve because, like Dr Norman Vincent Peale, church minister and author of *The Power of Positive Thinking*, you know that you are shooting for the moon and not the stars. You will also understand that when you are stepping into your greatness, the process is more important than the outcome. But you are not stopping here. You want to climb more steps.

In the fifth step to greatness, you are going to use the V.I.S.I.O.N© system as your vehicle to travel to another hemisphere with a different time zone where your dreams are possible. While there, you are going to realise that it is better to live from imagination and not memory. You are going to have the chance to visualise inside your mind with your senses and imagine overcoming obstacles with no fear. The V.I.S.I.O.N© system is going to allow you to have in your mind what you want while knowing, like Napoleon Hill, author and founder of *The Science of Success*, that whatever your mind can conceive and believe, it can achieve. But you are not stopping here. You are climbing further to the next step.

Public speaker and networker Porter Gale named her book: *Your Network is Your Net Worth*. In the sixth step to greatness, you are going to dedicate your time to reviewing your network using the P.E.O.P.L.E© model. You have the chance to ask these questions about the people you associate with. What are they bringing into my life? Are they purposeful? Are they encouraging? Are they opportunity experts? Are they productive? Are they living full? Are they exemplary? You are going to ask more questions: Do they fuel or empty my life? Do they inspire me to become the best version of me? Do they ignite my heart? Do they empower me? You are going to ask even more and more questions: what am I becoming emotionally, academically, financially, and spiritually because of these people? Upon answering these questions, you are going to attract more great people into your life and repel toxic people from your life.  But you are not going to stop here. You are going to take all that you have and all that you are with you to the final step.

Have you ever seen someone standing by the corner of a street and wondering how to cross to the other side? At one point in our life, we are standing at the corner of the street waiting for someone to lead us across. In the seventh step to greatness, you are going to complete activities that are going to help you move you from the street corner. You are going to follow the incredible A.C.T.I.O.N© system to finally step into your greatness. The A.C.T.I.O.N© system is going to allow you emulate great people and ask important questions about your life, your dreams, and your goals. You are not going to leave the questions unanswered. You are to embark on the road to educate yourself because you know quality education is food for your mind. You are going to be committed to doing whatever it takes to have what you want.

Reaching the seventh step to greatness is the end of this workbook but it is not the end of you. It is the end of the *7 Steps to Greatness* but it is not the end of your journey to greatness. You are invited to increase your action as you cruise on the motorway to your greatness forever. And now, it is time for you to start with the activities in the first step to greatness. I believe in you. I believe in your dreams. I believe in your potential to live a great life. Let us go and give it all.

# STEP 1: FIND YOURSELF

'Our deepest fear is not that we are inadequate. Our deepest fear is that we are powerful beyond measure. It is our light, not our darkness that most frightens us. We ask ourselves, "Who am I to be brilliant, gorgeous, talented, fabulous?" Actually, who are you not to be? You are a child of God. Your playing small does not serve the world. There is nothing enlightened about shrinking so that other people won't feel insecure around you. We are all meant to shine, as children do. We were born to make manifest the glory of God that is within us. It's not just in some of us; it's in everyone. And as we let our own light shine, we unconsciously give other people permission to do the same. As we are liberated from our own fear, our presence automatically liberates others'.

Marianne Williamson

# Who am I?

Thank you reading my bestselling book *7 Steps to Greatness: The Masterplan to Take Your Life, Studies, Career and Business to the Next Level*. You have been so courageous and taken the first step to your greatness. Before you proceed onto the activities in this workbook, I would like to ask you some questions. Are you ready to discover more about yourself?  Are you ready to give birth to A NEW YOU? To discover yourself and give birth to a new you, you must be HUNGRY. Deep hunger will allow you to find yourself. Deep hunger will allow you to live your dreams. Like you, I have been HUNGRY. Do you remember my story?

*In Summer 2017, my wife and I were hungry to achieve our dream as international speakers and coaches. Our hunger put us on a journey from London in England to Miami in Florida for a life changing mentorship programme with Les Brown - the world's number one motivational speaker. This journey took a lot of time to prepare, a lot of resources and energy from us. As we travelled via Toronto, we met a lot of amazing people we had never seen before and went through a lot of new places we have never been before. Going through these various 21st Century airports, border posts with cutting age technology and patiently waiting in the mazy queues, I was touched by many questions asked of me and of other passengers by the immigration officers. One of the questions was: **Who are you?***

Over time, it became clear that if my wife and I wanted to arrive at our destination, we needed to honestly answer the questions asked of us. As you travel to your greatness, as you go through the various border posts in your life, as you patiently queue with deep hunger to live a great life, I want you to answer the question: **Who am I?** As you ponder on this question, remember the ancient Philosopher Socrates' dictum, **'Know thyself for the unexamined life is not worth living'.** I now invite you to say, **'My unexamined life is not worth living today, I must know myself'.**

## Write

What comes to your mind when you hear the word **'ME'**? With conviction, write 7 words that best describe you today.

1. ________________________________________________________________

2. ________________________________________________________________

3. ________________________________________________________________

4. ________________________________________________________________

5. ________________________________________________________________

6. ________________________________________________________________

7. ________________________________________________________________

## Visualise

This is who you are today. Visualise yourself with all your senses the person you are.  See yourself being fully alive through the words you used to describe yourself. Now put your photograph or draw with great creativity a sketch of yourself below. Locate, where in your opinion, what you mentioned in the previous activity is. Is there any part of you that is missing? Add it on.

## What are my unique qualities?

Do you remember the miracle power within you? Richard Collier says, **'Always there is something within you urging you on to bigger things, giving you no peace, no rest, no chance to be lazy…This "something" within you keeps telling you that you can do anything you want to do, be anything you want to be, have anything you want to have…'**. What is it? Kurt Hahn says, **'There is more in us that we know. If we can be made to see it, perhaps, for the rest of our lives, we will be unwilling to settle for less'**. In my opinion, the more in you is expressed by your qualities and characteristics.

Have you taken time to search the more inside of you or you are pre-occupied with the outside. I invite you to take time and examine your life now. There is an old Sufi story about a man who had lost the keys to his house. He started searching outside his house under the bright streetlights that lit the road near to his house. Many neighbours joined him to look for the keys. After sometime, one of the neighbours asked, 'Where did you lose your keys?'. The man replied, 'Inside my house'. Amazed, the neighbour asked, 'Then why are we looking out here?' The man replied, 'Because there's more light out here'. It might be the time to look in the dark places to find yourself for without the darkness, you won't be able to see the light. **Where are the keys to your life? Which dark places in your life might give you a clue of who you are?**

## Write

What are your unique qualities? How different are you from other people?
What do your friends or other people notice about you? Write down 7 qualities
you possess.

1. ______________________________________________________

2. ______________________________________________________

3. ______________________________________________________

4. ______________________________________________________

5. ______________________________________________________

6. ______________________________________________________

7. ______________________________________________________

Now imagine that you are excelling in all these qualities. see yourself applying
them in all areas of your life and say to yourself and mean it, **'My life is
blossoming in total perfection'**.

# What are my gifts?

You can get all that you want in any area of your life if you tap into your gifts. Your gifts will take you to many places through the avenues you could ever imagine. People who do not know the value of their gifts are easy prey and end up walking in the dark alleys of life. I am reminded of Jomo Kenyatta in his book Facing Mount Kenya where he writes: **'When the missionaries arrived, the Africans had the land and the missionaries had the Bible. They taught us how to pray with eyes closed. When we opened them, they had the land and we had the Bible'**. These people in Africa had a treasure in their hands but they did not know it. They did not use it. However, the missionaries knew it, and used it. This is the situation that some of us are in. **Which treasures do you have and not currently using? What is stopping you? Who is stealing your treasures from you? What can you do about it?**

## Discover

The theologian Hans von Balthasar is saying to you today, **'What you are is God's gift to you, what you become is your gift to God'**. Take a look at who you are: a gift to the world.  How do you manifest your life as a gift? What are the good things that you involve yourself in that make the world proud of you? In other words, what are your gifts? What are your talents?  What are your interests and hobbies? Now make a list all the things that come to your mind. Be proud of your gifts because these are the assets of YOU.

1. ______________________________

2. ______________________________

3. ______________________________

4. ______________________________

5. ______________________________

6. ______________________________

7. ______________________________

8. ______________________________

9. ______________________________

10. ______________________________

11. ______________________________

12. ______________________________

13. ______________________________

14. ______________________________

## Give thanks

What a cherished gift you are. Think of all those people that are not able to do the things that you can do: walk, talk, read, smile, and many others. Take time and recollect the things that you are thankful today.

_______________________________________________

_______________________________________________

_______________________________________________

_______________________________________________

_______________________________________________

_______________________________________________

_______________________________________________

_______________________________________________

_______________________________________________

_______________________________________________

_______________________________________________

_______________________________________________

Give thanks. You might wish to use this prayer these affirmations: **The light of God surrounds me. The love of God enfolds me. The power of God flows through me. Wherever I am, God is, and all is well. I am blessed and highly favoured.**

# Let go or be dragged

Get the idea that life could be different for you if you decided to go beyond yourself, beyond your body, and go beyond your statue. In my book '*7 Steps to Greatness*', you read a reflection from the world's foremost spiritual guru Anthony de Mello about your statue.

> *A sculptor has been making a statue of you. The statue is ready and you go to his studio to have a look at it before it appears in public. He gives you the key to the room where your statue is so that you can see it for yourself and take all the time you want to examine it alone.*
>
> *You open the door. The room is dark. There, in the middle of the room is your statue, covered with a cloth... You walk up to the statue and take the cloth off...Then you step back and look at your statue. What is your first impression?...Are you pleased or dissatisfied?...Notice the material it is made of...Walk around it...see it from different angles...Look at it from far, then come closer and look at the details...Touch the statue... notice whether it is rough or smooth... cold or warm to the touch. What parts of the statue do you like?...What parts of the statue do you dislike?...*
>
> *Say something to your statue...What does the statue reply?...What do you say in return?...What do you say in return? Keep on speaking as long as you or the statue have something to say...Now become the statue...What does it feel like to be your statue?...What kind of existence do you have as the statue?'*

The author John Mason named his book *You Were Born an Original. Don't Die a Copy.* Decide from today to live an original life. Say today, **'I have got myself into this copy. It is only me who can get myself out of it. I am not going to be a volunteer victim. I am going to live an original life'**.

## Offload

Reflect on your own life and think about the things that you need to unload so that you can live an original life. This is the life you are meant to live. Write down these on a separate piece of paper or down here. These are the things that are holding you back and slowing down your growth. Start getting rid of them in your life. They have squatted your life for long. You deserve your life back.

1. ______________________________

2. ______________________________

3. ______________________________

4. ______________________________

5. ______________________________

6. ______________________________

7. ______________________________

## Upload

What type of person do you want to become? How do you want to change? What are the things you need to improve on? Do you tend to make excuses rather than accept responsibility? Do you spend too much time talking and not doing? Do you procrastinate a lot? On the lines below, list 7 qualities that you need to improve on or attract into your life.

1. ______________________________________________

2. ______________________________________________

3. ______________________________________________

4. ______________________________________________

5. ______________________________________________

6. ______________________________________________

7. ______________________________________________

Keep this list handy so that you can check on it every day to see how closer you are getting to a NEW YOU. Start working on the first one today.

# A New Me

Now imagine that you have improved all areas of your life. You have achieved all your dreams and your life's purpose. In the box below, describe or draw the NEW YOU fully alive and great. Alternatively, put a photograph of your happiest moment in life so far.

# Believe

Liked Anthony de Mello, affirm, **'I have a treasure: the thing that I value most in life. I relive the events that led me to discover it. I think of the history of my life from the time I found this treasure...what it has done and meant to me. I stand before this treasure and I say, "Of all the things I have, you are the dearest"...I am a treasure. Someday, somewhere, someone discovered me. I should have no awareness of my worth if someone had not found it. I recall and relive the details of the finding and I am a multifaceted treasure'**

## Do

**Create** *time and space within you*

- ✓ Find a quiet space inside your and outside of you

- ✓ Journey to a special place in your heart

- ✓ Sit down and relax

- ✓ Take time to be you

**Review** *who you are*

- ✓ Start off an inner conversation with yourself

- ✓ Be grateful of who you are today

- ✓ Appreciate who you are: miracle, uncommon, and gift

**Reflect** *about where you have been with your life*

- ✓ Why am I the person I am today?

- ✓ What drives me? What inhibits me?

- ✓ Am I happy with what is happening in my life today?

- ✓ Why am I not where I want to be with my life?

- ✓ What are the things I need to offload/ upload into my life?

**Visualise** *your future*

- ✓ When I offload/ upload these things I will see...

- ✓ I will feel...

- ✓ I will touch...

- ✓ I will smell...

- ✓ I will taste...

**Affirm** *who you are and what you want*

- ✓ I am a miracle in action

- ✓ I am a gift with infinite gifts

- ✓ There is greatness within me

- ✓ I am committed to achieving my greatness

- ✓ I am going to make my life a masterpiece

**Take** *action*

✓ Choose three areas in your life that you are going to be great in today

_______________________________________________

_______________________________________________

_______________________________________________

✓ In order to achieve my greatness today I am going to...

_______________________________________________

_______________________________________________

_______________________________________________

# STEP 2: DISCOVER YOUR PURPOSE

**'The two most important days in your life are the day you are born and the day you find out why'. Mark Twain**

# What is the purpose of my life?

I am glad you have taken time to know who you are. It is now time for you to use who you are to get what you want from life.  In my book *7 Steps to Greatness*, you imagined a recently discovered country. This country had a lot of untapped resources. You were given the task to organise the delivery of good and services to your citizens. You wished to have your country become the most powerful in the world. How did you do it? What name did you give to your country?  Did you struggle finding a name? You and me agreed that the country was YOU. Can you believe it?

You are the country. You have a lot of untapped resources that will make you great. You want to unleash your greatness. How are you going to do it? In this step, I am going to help you tap into your resources. The key is discovering your purpose.   Your purpose is your **'WHY'** in life. Your purpose is what is going to help you get what you want from life. It is the foundation for your life since without it your life would have no meaning. It is your vision for being in this universe. One of my favourite books says, 'Where there is no vision, the people perish'. This means your vision is your why for living. It also means if you have no vision of yourself, you have nothing to live for.

## Develop

What is the purpose of your life? Why are you here? What is your personal mission? How will future generations know that your life was worth living? What is the vision for your life? What inspires you to get into action, be in action and to stay in action? In the space below, write your purpose or mission statement for your life. Write in in the presence so that it is being accomplished in your mind. Here is my vision as an example:

**'I am a pencil in the hand of God. I am writing three chapters with my life. I am instrument of peace in the world. I am a channel of hope in peoples' hearts. I am a messenger of greatness in the world'.**

## Deepen

What you just have written is your Satnav through the interlocking streets of life. Though most people use a Satnav when they are driving from A to B, they rarely have a Satnav for their own life! They do not see where their life is going, a dangerous way of living. Like driving aimlessly without a Satnav is dangerous, so is living without a vision. An African proverb says, **'If you don't stand for something, you will fall for anything'**. I do not wish this to happen to you. From today, decide to firmly hold your vision. Let it be the ground of your being. Allow your vision to be your magnificent obsession. Deep your belief in you and live for your vision.

Helen Keller says 'The only thing worse than being blind is having sight but no vision'. Let me share my vision again. **'I am a pencil in the hand of God. I am writing three chapters with my life. I am instrument of peace in the world. I am a channel of hope in peoples' hearts. I am a messenger of greatness in the world'**. I am sharing my vision with you, not to impress you but to impress upon you. As you can see, your vision needs to be magnetic, compelling and bigger than you. It needs to be magnetic so that it is always attracting you and others towards its realisation. Your vision needs to attract people, circumstances and resources that will make it possible. Your vision will align the universe to your side. It needs to be compelling so that it repels the hurricanes and tough times in your life.

# Increase

Before moving on to the next point, let me share with you one of the deepest secrets: **your level of belief is directly proportional to what you can make happen**. So, the more you believe, the more you will actualise your purpose.  The lesser you belief the lesser you will achieve your vision. What is the size of your vision? Do you have a mentor to help you enlarge your vision? Why? Why not?

People who have found their purpose or vision are uncommon. They live, see, and act differently. You will experience this when you find your purpose. Like them, your heart will pump with purpose and not blood. Your eyes will not see random events but visions of a better future for you, for your family and for the rest of the universe. Your ears will hear not the noises of distractions but the calling to greatness. You will allow your feet not to walk anywhere but to where your treasure is hidden. You will walk with purpose. You will eat with purpose. You will sleep with purpose. You will talk with purpose. You will hear with purpose. You will see with purpose. What a transformed human being you will become. What a great life you will aim for once you have found your WHY for living. So, increase the level of your belief and enlarge your vision. Take time and describe your enlarged vision on the next page.

# My Large vision

# Do

**Create** *time and space within you*

- ✓ Find a quiet space inside your and outside of you
- ✓ Journey to a special place in your heart
- ✓ Sit down and relax
- ✓ Take time to be you

**Review** *who you are*

- ✓ Start off an inner conversation with yourself
- ✓ Be grateful of who you are today
- ✓ Appreciate who you are: miracle, uncommon, and gift

**Reflect** *on your purpose*

- ✓ What is the purpose of my life?
- ✓ Why am I alive?
- ✓ What do I really want from life?
- ✓ What is my personal mission?

**Visualise** *your future*

- ✓ See your vision: the foundation for your life

✓ Imagine digging the trenches and laying the foundation for your life

✓ Feel, smell, touch, taste, see what your vision

✓ Appreciate the great and hard work you have done

✓ Notice how positive you feel about yourself

**Affirm** *who you are and what you want*

✓ My time has come to live my vision

✓ Good things are supposed to happen to me

✓ No matter how bad it is or how worse it gets, I am going to make it

✓ I can do everything with... who strengthens me.

**Take** *action*

✓ Create a vision board

✓ Use your vision board as a visual reminder of your WHY

# Hold

Like Robert Collier, '**Hold in your mind the thing you most desire. Affirm it. Believe it to be an existing fact.... You can have anything you want - if you want it badly enough... Your desire must be visualised, must be persisted in, must be concentrated upon, must be impressed upon your subconscious mind. ... If you can visualise the thing you want, if you can impress upon your subconscious mind the belief that you have it, you can safely leave to it the finding of the means of getting it...'**

# STEP 3: DREAM WHILE AWAKE

'All men dream, but not all equally. Those who dream by night, in the dusty recesses of their minds, wake to find it was all vanity. But the dreamers of the day are dangerous, for they may act on their dreams with open eyes, and make things happen' T. E. Lawrence

# Do you hear your dreams calling you?

When I was young I used to have a lot of dreams in my sleep. I dreamt flying in the clouds like a bird and enjoying the view from above. I dreamt of running as lions chased me and suddenly waking up before they caught me. I dreamt of sharing my favourite meal as I visited relatives and enjoyed being in their presence. I dreamt of the games I had during the day and how I did not want them to end. I had all these and many other dreams while I was asleep. Like me, you probably had similar dreams while you were in your subconscious state. These are only a small percentage of the dreams that took place while in our subconscious state as most of our dreams went unnoticed.

Nowadays, I have different dreams. I am now aware of all my dreams and most of them are becoming true. This has been possible because I have climbed the first steps and taken time to know myself and discover my purpose. You too have taken the same steps and you should be noticing that the way you dream is changing. You must have started dreaming while you are awake because, unlike many people, you are uncommon and you possess miracle power to do so. If you have not yet started, you are going to dream when you are fully conscious and remember all your dreams. You are going to take James Dean's advice and 'dream as if you'll live forever, live as if you'll die today'.

## Where do your dreams come from?

I told you this story about the source of my dreams in my book *7 Steps to Greatness*. We had just finished eating our dinner in the back courtyard under the light of the moon. Like every other night, we were getting ready to sleep. Suddenly there was noise and gunshots outside. With my parents and two elder brothers, we had to leave our house by the back door and run to the banana plantations. That was the beginning of a long night that I spent in the banana plantations when rebels attacked my village. When we came back in the morning, part of our house was destroyed, my parents' shop was burgled and my school had become an army barracks. I remember my family and many other people travelling in refugee truck being displaced to another village. That was the start of a life without school living in a different village with different people. This was the start of me dreaming while I was awake.

I was defined by this moment in Uganda. It brought me very close to my purpose and showed me the vision of what I wanted to create for me and my country. I felt called by something within me to use my life as an instrument of peace and a channel of hope beyond the war zone I was living in. At a time this seemed like an impossible mission, how was I to achieve my purpose? How was I to live my vision? For this to happen, I had not only let the moment define me but I defined the moment. Though I was living in war during those years, I did not let war live in me. It was an opportunity for me to dream while I was awake. During the one year while I was out of school, I dreamt of going back to school and completing my education. I dreamt of completing my education in a world class university, teaching about peace, and writing stories that restored hope in people. In this example, you can see how my dreams are linked to my purpose - being an instrument of peace in the world.

## Build

Revisit your purpose which is the foundation for your life. Think about your dreams which is the roof for the life you are building. During war and out of school, my dream was to get education and fulfil my vision of being an instrument of peace. **Reflect on your life now, what are your dreams?**

## Dream big

In the second step to greatness, I encouraged you to have a large vision. In this third step, I now encourage you to dream big. If you have a limited vision for your life, your dreams too will be small. When you have a large vision, you require big dreams. Your big dreams and large vision will shelter you from the storms of life. In his book *As a Man Thinketh*, James Allen writes, **'The dreamers are the saviours of the world'**. You can only be a saviour of the world when you have big dreams. It is possible for you to have big dreams too. So, decide to dream big from today. Become a big dreamer. Ask yourself: **how big are my dreams?  Are my dreams going to be left undone when I leave this planet? Can my dreams become my legacy?** Take a moment and amend your dreams.

______________________________________

______________________________________

______________________________________

______________________________________

______________________________________

______________________________________

______________________________________

______________________________________

## Sacrifice

Big dreams require sacrifice. My parents' dream was education. They believed education was the only ticket out of poverty for their children. As a result, they worked day and night to make their dream become true. They struggled to get fees so that my siblings and I received a good education. I vividly remember when my father got into debt due to paying our school fees. One of the people whom he had borrowed money from took legal action and he was imprisoned. After two weeks in a prison cell, one of our family friends gave money to him so that he could be released. But as it was the start of the new school term and I had to go to school, he chose to stay in prison so that I could have the money to pay off my school fees. My father stayed in prison for his dream. He sacrificed his freedom so that I received education. What an uncommon way to live his dream. My question to you is: **what are you prepared to sacrifice so that you live your dreams?**

___________________________________________

___________________________________________

___________________________________________

___________________________________________

___________________________________________

___________________________________________

___________________________________________

# Work

Though we were materially poor, we did not let poverty live in us. We were rich because we had big dreams. Like my parents, I believed that it was possible to achieve my dreams. Like my parents, I decided that education was my only road out of poverty. From an early age, I decided to get the highest form of education so that I became a symbol of education greatness in my family. Since I had received the gift of education, my dream was to give the gift of education to my siblings and to those who crossed my path. As a result, my school holidays were not spent watching TV or playing computer games. I spent my holidays working at my local church so that I could get money to pay for my education. In the hot sunshine of Uganda, I slashed the church compound and worked on the church farm. There were times when I was asked to teach my local language to the American missionaries who came to visit my church parish. Like my parents, no matter how hard it was or worse it got, I did not lose sight of my big dream. My question to you is: are you prepared to never lose sight of your dreams?

_______________________________________________________________

_______________________________________________________________

_______________________________________________________________

_______________________________________________________________

_______________________________________________________________

_______________________________________________________________

## Starve your fears

Sorry I have taken a lot of your time talking about the dreams I have had while awake. My intention is to show you how I have lived my dreams against the odds. My intention is to help you realise that when you dream big, obstacles become insignificant. Take time to reflect about your situation now since you may be having your own challenges. How are you starving your fears?

_______________________________________________

_______________________________________________

_______________________________________________

_______________________________________________

_______________________________________________

_______________________________________________

_______________________________________________

_______________________________________________

_______________________________________________

_______________________________________________

_______________________________________________

_______________________________________________

_______________________________________________

# Fight

It took me over 20 years to achieve my dream of getting a PhD: the highest form of education I desired. I can say that my life would have been different had my parents not held onto their dream of education.  However, too many people give up and don't fight for their dreams like you and me. They get scared and stop craving for their dreams when they face obstacles. As Les Brown says, **'Too many of us are not living our dream because we are living our fears'**. The choice is yours: live your dreams or live your fears. Do you want to live your dreams or your fears? Are your past failures hindering you to fight for your dreams?  How are you fighting for your dreams? Remember, when you stop fighting for what you want, what you don't want takes over. So, continue fighting for what you want no matter what happens in your life.

# The fire within

Les Brown says, **'There comes a time when you have to drop your burdens in order to fight for yourself and your dreams'**. The time is now. Wanting your dreams is not enough. Having dreams is not enough. Being hungry for your dreams is not enough. You must crave your dream. Refuse to fall behind in your dreams. There is a huge fire burning inside of you. This fire is bigger than the fire that is burning outside of you. This fire is not going to allow you to settle in one place. This fire is going to make you climb the *7 Steps to Greatness*.   If you are not feeling the fire inside you, you have not yet got big dreams.

If you have not yet discovered big dreams, keep searching. As you search for your dreams, your dreams are seeking you too. Refuse to stand on the corner of the street and park yourself and your dreams. Give your dreams a chance to see the light of the day. Can you imagine looking back on your life only to discover you have not lived your dreams? Can you imagine reaching at the end of your life only to discover you are dying with your dreams? Henry David Thoreau says, **'Oh, God, to reach a point of death only to realise that you have never lived'**. It is a frightening thought, isn't it? Your dreams would say to you, **'we came to you so that you would give us life. You parked us on the motorway of life. You took away our life. Only you could have given us life. Now we are dying with you!'**

## Feed your dreams

Circumstances may be going against you but remember Socrates is saying to you now, **'no human condition is ever permanent'**. I would like you to imagine all your challenges gone and imagine living your wildest dream now. Use these affirmations to strengthen your beliefs and feed your dreams:

- ✓ It is possible I can live my dream.

- ✓ I must work on my dream every day.

- ✓ It is not over until I achieved my dream.

- ✓ I will fight for my dreams until I win.

- ✓ No matter how hard it is or bad it gets, I will live my dreams not my fears.

_______________________________________________

_______________________________________________

_______________________________________________

_______________________________________________

_______________________________________________

_______________________________________________

_______________________________________________

_______________________________________________

## Do

**Create** *time and space within you*

- ✓ Find a quiet space inside your and outside of you

- ✓ Journey to a special place in your heart

- ✓ Sit down and relax

- ✓ Take time to be you

**Review** *who you are*

- ✓ Start off an inner conversation with yourself

- ✓ Be grateful of who you are today

- ✓ Appreciate who you are: miracle, uncommon and a gift

- ✓ Reconsider your purpose and personal mission

**Reflect** *on your dreams*

- ✓ What is the dream for my life?

- ✓ Am I busy living my dreams or dying with my fears?

- ✓ What are my big or wildest dreams?

- ✓ What do I need to change in my life?

**Visualise** *your dreams*

- ✓ See your dreams: the roof for your vision

- ✓ Visualise yourself taking action and going after your dreams

- ✓ Feel, smell, touch, taste, and see your dreams come true

- ✓ Appreciate the great and hard work you have done

- ✓ Notice how positive you feel about yourself

**Affirm** *who you are, your purpose and dreams*

- ✓ I will work until I achieve my dreams.

- ✓ It is possible I can live my dreams.

- ✓ I must work on my dreams every day.

- ✓ It is not over until I achieve my dreams.

- ✓ I will fight for my dreams until I win.

- ✓ No matter how hard it is or bad it gets, I will live my dreams.

**Take** *action*

- ✓ Create and use a dream board

# STEP 4: DEVELOP STAR GOALS

'The tragedy of life doesn't lie in not reaching your goal. The tragedy lies in having no goal to reach'. Benjamin E Mays

# Are you ready?

What amazing success you have had since you started stepping into your greatness. You now know who you are. You know the purpose of your life. You have a lot of dreams that you want to accomplish before you leave this planet. You have been travelling to your greatness. You have now reached the point of no return on your journey. As you step onto this fourth step, you cannot afford to go back to who you were before with unclear vision and fuzzy dreams. The energy you have invested in your journey up to this point is greater than what you will need to reach your destination. You are like an athlete who can only focus on reaching the finishing line and winning the race.

On the finishing line is clearly marked WELCOME TO GREATNES. You can clearly see the great life you will live once you reach the finishing line. Now is the time for you to bridge the gap between what you have in your mind and want you want to manifest in reality.  It is time for you to choose a route that is going to take you to your dreams and design a plan of action.

# Desire

What do you want out of life? Write down what you really want to acquire, achieve or accomplish in these domains of your life? Start with these boxes and add in the last ones.

| Personal | Education |
|---|---|
| Relationships | Career |
| Cause? | Business? |
|  |  |

## Evaluate

What kind of person do you want to be? What type of career do you want? What type of business would like to be in?  How would you describe your dream job? How much are you willing to invest to get that job? What level of education do you aspire to? What qualification would you like to have? Which university would you like to go?

________________________________________

________________________________________

________________________________________

________________________________________

________________________________________

________________________________________

________________________________________

________________________________________

________________________________________

________________________________________

________________________________________

________________________________________

________________________________________

________________________________________

# Big goals

Goals are the reasons your dreams will stand or fall. To be able to achieve the big dreams you have, you need big goals. Goals are the pillars to your dreams. Goals are the fuel to your dreams. People who live without goals muddle through life without knowing where they are going. They sleep walk through life. Goals will help you move from your where you are now to where you want to go. Les Brown says, **'many people fail in life not because they aim too high and miss'**. Many people fail because they aim too low and hit'. How high are you aiming: too low or too high? Take time and adjust your goals to high for you have big dreams.

# S.T.A.R© goals?

Your purpose is the foundation for your life. You dreams form the roof for your life. Your goals are the pillars that link your roof to your foundation. They are the pillars that are planted in the foundation and hold the roof. If you are looking for pillars to build a durable house that will last, you need strong pillars. There are different types of pillars in the market. The type of pillars you use will determine how strong your house will last. Just as you would go for the best pillars to support your house, go for the best goals that will propel you to your dreams. While looking for goals, I found the best ones at the Les Brown Institute in Fort Lauderdale, Florida. They are called S.T.A.R© goals and have become the highway to my dreams. The acronym S.T.A.R© stands for:

- Strongly felt by you and connected to your dreams;

- Theatre of your mind;

- Absolutely necessary;

- Ridiculously hard to achieve.

Let us now take time and examine what each of these pillars represents and how they may help you live your dreams and not your fears.

## Strongly felt and connected

One of my favourite books says, 'for where your treasure is, there your heart will be also'. I believe your dreams are your treasures. Your goals need to go and be attached to your treasures in your heart. Your goals need to go and make the heart their domicile. If your goals are not strongly connected to your dreams in your heart, you will experience difficulties in achieving them. When difficulties come, you will give up because your heart is not connected to your goals and vice versa. Your goals must be everything to you. You must be willing to do whatever it takes to achieve them. You must be ready to move heaven and earth in order to achieve them. **How can you apply this to your dream today?**

My advice to you is that you must have goals that enable you to live your dreams not your fears. You have to want your goals badly enough that without them you cannot achieve your dreams. If your goals are strongly felt and connected to your dreams, you will be excited and on fire to achieve them. Your goals will fuel your dreams and increase your motivation. You will wake up passionate about attaining them. If your goals are connected to your heart, you will feel them in your heart of hearts. Reflect on the extent to which your goals are connected to your heart. Write down what comes to your mind and to your heart here.

# In the theatre of your mind

Not only should your goals be strongly felt in your heart, they also need to be played out in the theatre of your mind. Before you can achieve your goals in reality, you must be able to visualise them vividly on the screen of your mind. You must be able to see them with clarity and how their successful completion will transform your life. I imagine Steve Jobs visualised the iPhone and other Apple products on the screen of his mind before producing them as physical products that have now transformed people's lives all over the world.

It is only when we see our goals on the screen of our minds that we believe they are possible. So, picture your goals in your mind every day. Close your eyes and see your future self, future day to day activities, future business, future foundations, future bank accounts, future life and future personal economy. Let your mind become the theatre where the videos of your goals are played. Your videos could include being approved for a loan to complete your education; paying off your mortgage so that you own your home; travelling the world in a cruise and enjoying your retirement; starting a business and being financially free; writing your book and becoming a bestselling author.

What strategies are you going to apply so that you see your goals in your mind?

_______________________________________________________________

_______________________________________________________________

_______________________________________________________________

_______________________________________________________________

# Absolutely necessary

You now know that your goals need to be felt in your heart and visible on the screen of your mind. The third feature of S.T.A.R© goals is that they are absolutely necessary. This means your goals are a life-and-death issue to you. That was what my father did when he chose to stay in prison and give me the money which was to buy his freedom so that I can use it to pay school fees. For my father, my freedom from ignorance was greater than his freedom from prison. From this experience, I learnt that if I was ever to live my dreams, I needed to make my goals absolutely necessary. Now write 7 reasons why you think you deserve your goals. For example, I have put up with enough hard times and I now earn the right to expect more from life.

______________________________________________

______________________________________________

______________________________________________

______________________________________________

______________________________________________

______________________________________________

______________________________________________

______________________________________________

______________________________________________

______________________________________________

______________________________________________

In my book *7 Steps to Greatness*, I told you about my wife and I searching for a house. On a deeper level, I realised that there were other universal laws that were working on our behalf beyond our determination. One of them was that stated by the 13th Century Persian Poet Rumi that **'what you seek is seeking you'**. So, as we searched for the house, there were people and circumstances that were put in place so that we got what we were seeking.

So, as you move towards your dreams, make your goals absolutely necessary that if they are not achieved, then your life will cease to continue. Once the universe notices your determination, it will give you support so that you get what you want from life.

# Ridiculously hard to achieve

In this last feature of S.T.A.R© goals, I urge you to make your goals hard to achieve. This is probably what Dr Normal Vincent Peale meant by saying, **'Shoot for the moon and even if you miss, you will land among the stars'**. This is what possibly what Les Brown means when he says, **'Most people fail in life not because they aim too high and miss, but because they aim too low and hit'**. If your goals are too easy, then you might end up failing. If your goals are too hard, even if you miss, you will have learnt from the process. The process of striving to achieve your goals is more important than achieving your goals. So, shoot for the moon. Have tough goals that will keep you inspired. Have goals that will keep you focused. Look at your life now. What is blocking you from setting hard goals?

__________________________________________________________________

__________________________________________________________________

__________________________________________________________________

__________________________________________________________________

__________________________________________________________________

__________________________________________________________________

__________________________________________________________________

__________________________________________________________________

__________________________________________________________________

__________________________________________________________________

# You deserve

You deserve your dreams.  If you are going to live your dreams, you have to see it for yourself. If you can't see it for yourself, why should others see it for you? You have to have high expectations for your own life and your development. Here are 7 questions to help you progress steadily towards what you deserve:

1. Think about the various domains of your life such as business, studies, career, relationships, and many others. Ask yourself: What must I become?

What do I value most? Wealth? Health?  Adventure? Personal growth? Career? Family? Fame? Education?  Relationships? Respect? charity? Write what I value most here and why.

__________________________________________________

__________________________________________________

__________________________________________________

__________________________________________________

__________________________________________________

__________________________________________________

__________________________________________________

__________________________________________________

__________________________________________________

__________________________________________________

__________________________________________________

__________________________________________________

__________________________________________________

__________________________________________________

__________________________________________________

Is what I value aligned with whom I want to become? Rank what I value above in the order of importance. What are my 5 most important valuables?

_________________________________________

_________________________________________

_________________________________________

_________________________________________

_________________________________________

_________________________________________

_________________________________________

_________________________________________

_________________________________________

_________________________________________

_________________________________________

_________________________________________

_________________________________________

2. Are my goals established in the future? Are they an extension of my values? Can I visualise them now and see how they will look like once I have achieved them?

_______________________________________________

_______________________________________________

_______________________________________________

_______________________________________________

_______________________________________________

_______________________________________________

_______________________________________________

_______________________________________________

_______________________________________________

_______________________________________________

_______________________________________________

_______________________________________________

_______________________________________________

_______________________________________________

_______________________________________________

_______________________________________________

3.  What is my most important goal now?

| **My goal is** | | |
| --- | --- | --- |
| _____________________________________ | | |
| I will do | I will find key people | By this target date |
| | | |
| | | |
| | | |

**Do:** Go out and pursue your goals because you deserve.

4. Do I have a motivation plan? Motivation does not come naturally to all. It can be learned and developed through believing in yourself, overcoming fear, using mistakes and failures to build, and immediacy: starting now. What must I believe in order to meet each goal?

What turns my fear, stress, anxiety into power?

How will I learn from my mistakes and failures and forget about them once I know what to do next?

How will I eliminate procrastination from my life once and for all?

5. Is there enough discipline in my life now? How can I manage myself better today? How will I stay flexible and embrace change in the days ahead?

____________________________________________________________________

____________________________________________________________________

____________________________________________________________________

____________________________________________________________________

____________________________________________________________________

____________________________________________________________________

____________________________________________________________________

____________________________________________________________________

____________________________________________________________________

____________________________________________________________________

____________________________________________________________________

____________________________________________________________________

____________________________________________________________________

____________________________________________________________________

____________________________________________________________________

____________________________________________________________________

6. What are my next steps after reaching my goals?  How will I make sure that my goals are aligned to my dreams and focused on what I want?

_______________________________________________________________

# Review

You now know how S.T.A.R© goals can help you reach your dreams. As you journey to your greatness, use goals that you feel in your heart and are visible on the screen of your mind. As you strive to live your dreams, have goals that are life and death issue to you: goals that stretch you to the limits of your existence. As you build your dreams, have goals that are strong enough to support them and push you towards the stars. As you journey to your dreams, have goals that will drive you to a higher purpose. As you crave for your dreams, have a mentor to help you lock your goals into your heart and write them on the screen of your mind. This way, you will live your dreams and not your fears. This way, you will step into your greatness and not forever stay in your comfort zone. Practice using S.T.A.R© goals every day.

# Do

**Create** *time and space within you*

- ✓ Find a quiet space inside your and outside of you

- ✓ Journey to a special place in your heart

- ✓ Sit down and relax

- ✓ Take time to be you

**Review** *who you are*

- ✓ Start off with an inner conversation with yourself

- ✓ Be grateful of who you are today

- ✓ Admire your purpose and your dreams in life

**Reflect** *on your goals*

- ✓ As you reflect on your goals, ask the following questions

- ✓ What are my top 3 goals?

- ✓ What do I expect out of these goals?

- ✓ What do I need to change in my life to achieve my goals?

- ✓ What actions am I going to do now? Next week? Next month? Next year?

**Visualise** *your goals*

- ✓ See your vision: the foundation for your life

- ✓ See your dreams: the roof for your foundation

- ✓ See your STAR goals: the pillars to your dreams

- ✓ Feel, smell, touch, taste, see your goals

- ✓ Visualise yourself taking massive action

- ✓ Appreciate the hard work you have done so far

- ✓ Notice how positive you feel about yourself

**Affirm** *who you are and what you want*

- ✓ **'If I want a thing bad enough I have to go out and fight for it, to work day and night for it, to give up my time, my peace and my sleep for it… If all that I dream and scheme is about it, and life seems useless and worthless without it… If I gladly sweat for it and fret for it and plan for it and lose all my terror of the opposition for it…If I simply go after that thing I want with all my capacity, strength and sagacity, faith, hope and confidence and stern pertinacity… If neither cold, poverty, famine nor gout, sickness nor pain of body and brain, can beset it, with the help of God, I WILL get it!'** Adapted from Berton Braley

**Take** *action*

- ✓ Add STAR goals to your vision board

- ✓ Create a plan of action for each goal

- ✓ Attend a goal setting workshop

# STEP 5: SEE WITH VISION

'The only thing worse than being blind is having sight but no vision'. Helen Keller

# Do you see with vision?

By now you know what you want from life. You want to make your vision a reality. You want to live your dreams and achieve your STAR goals. For this to happen in reality, you need to clearly see it in your mind first. Napoleon Hill says, **'Whatever the mind of man can conceive and believe, it can achieve'**. So, the ability to see what you want from life is essential to getting what you want from life. This is called visualisation: a method for programming your mind to see with clarity your vision, your dreams, and your goals. In this fifth step to greatness, I am giving you a V.I.S.I.O.N© that will help you see what you want from life. The acronym V.I.S.I.O.N© stands for:

- ✓ **V**isualise

- ✓ **I**nside the mind

- ✓ **S**enses

- ✓ **I**magine

- ✓ **O**vercome obstacles

- ✓ **N**o fear

To help you remember this **V.I.S.I.O.N©**, I urge you to learn this sentence: **I Visualise Inside** my mind with my **Senses** and I **Imagine Overcoming** obstacles with **N**o fear. Let us now explore each feature of this V.I.S.I.O.N©.

# Visualise

You might have already heard about visualisation. Shakti Gawain says that visualization: **'involves understanding the natural principles that govern the workings of our universe, and learning to use these principles in the most conscious and creative ways'**. Visualisation gives you the power to make events and circumstances real in your mind.

You can visualise what you want in any domain of your life: cooking, sports, prayer, marriage, education, business, etc. Research shows that successful men and women use visualisation to get what they want from life. For example, athletes visualise themselves winning the race before they even run the race. Footballers visualise themselves winning the match before they play it. This means the race or the match is won first in the mind before it is worn in reality. This implies winning the race or playing the match in reality is only a formality.

# Think

What 3 things do you want to do and be remembered for?

1. _______________________________________________________________

2. _______________________________________________________________

3. _______________________________________________________________

## Inside the mind

This is the second aspect of your V.I.S.I.O.N©. It is in the mind where visualisation takes place. Robert Collier says, **'We can do only what we think we can do. We can be only what we think we can be. We can have only what we think we can have. What we do, what we are, what we have, all depend upon what we think. We can never express anything that we do not first have in mind. The secret of all power, all success, all riches, is in first thinking powerful thoughts, successful thoughts, and thoughts of wealth, of supply. We must build them in our own mind first'**. This means whatever we achieve as human beings we create them first as ideas. Plato refers to this as the world of forms: a world that contains ideals of that which has the potential to exist in the material world. So, here the artist finds the idea of a portrait before painting it. A singer gets the idea of the song before singing it. An author gets the idea of a book before writing it. An inventor has the idea of an iPhone before making it. And you have the idea of your greatest life before you can live it. In truth, our ideas are blueprints that eventually become reality outside our minds when we act upon them. What ideas are coming to your mind right now?

_______________________________________________

_______________________________________________

_______________________________________________

_______________________________________________

_______________________________________________

# Senses

Senses are the doors to your mind. They help you access your mind faster so that you can see, smell, touch, feel, and taste what you want. You are where you are today because of what you have seen, touched, smelt, tasted, and felt. If you change what you are experiencing with your senses today, your results will change too. Let me give you an example. I am currently using my senses to visualize and write this workbook. If I decided I am no longer going to commit my time to writing this book, you would not be reading it. Brian Tracy says, **'As you change your mental pictures on the inside, your world on the outside will begin to change to correspond to those pictures'**. If you change the movies playing on the screen of your mind today, your life will change too. What movies are you playing to yourself? Can you find great moments in your life that you can use to create other great moments?

____________________________________________________

____________________________________________________

____________________________________________________

____________________________________________________

____________________________________________________

____________________________________________________

____________________________________________________

# Imagine

Many people live from their memory most of the time. They let their past determine their present and future. They allow what has happened to determine what will happen. Albert Einstein says, **'imagination is more important than facts'**. This is because without imagination, it is difficult to creature a future. Do you remember what I said about ideas? Things exist as ideas first before they exist in reality. It is imagination which allows you to see the ideas on the screen of your mind. It is only after imagining that you are able to go on and create facts in your physical environment. For example, from an early age, I had the idea of becoming a missionary, I then became a missionary for 10 years. After that I had the idea of becoming a teacher. I have been a teacher for the past 10 years. I then got the idea of becoming an entrepreneur and have been for the past 5 years. Then, I got the idea of becoming an international speaker, bestselling author and greatness coach. I am doing this now. As you can see from my own personal experience, without having the ideas and imagining those ideas becoming a reality first, I would not be who I am today. Without living from my imagination, I would be behind with my dreams and my goals.

In *Secret of the Ages*, James Allen says, **'Let a man alter his thoughts, and he will be astonished at the rapid transformation it will effect in the material conditions of his life'**. So, change your thoughts, change your life. What are your dominant thought right now? Is it a new job? Is it buying a new home? Is it improving your memory?

If you imagine the reality you want to create, you have the miracle power to manifest it in reality.

# Overcome obstacles

As you focus on your vision, you will experience a lot of obstacles. People with disappoint you and you will experience a lot of distractions. A lot of unexpected things will happen on the way to your greatness. What will you do? T Harv Eker says **'Rich people focus on opportunities. Poor people focus on obstacles'.** I would say that in moments of obstacles, people who are stepping into their greatness focus on opportunities and not obstacles.

Having the ability to see opportunities in the perceived obstacles will allow you to work towards getting what you want from life. This is what will separate you from the common people. This is what will distinguish you as someone who lives their dreams from those who live their fears.

You will therefore need to have control over what you are visualizing in a given situation. Do not let obstacles get on the way to your greatness. You have complete control of what you want from life and there is no one stopping you but you. Look back where you are in your life. Whatever you have achieved or not achieved is a product of how you have dealt with the obstacles which have come on your way. There are moments you have let obstacles get on your way and you have given up. There are also moments when you have not let obstacles get in the way to living your dreams. Can you recollect these moments when you have refused to give in to obstacles?

Do: Use these best moments to create your future success.

# No fear

You have now developed the skills to visualise in your mind and with your senses what you want from life. You have realized that you are likely to meet obstacles on the way to your dreams. Your approach is going to be searching for opportunities in every perceived obstacles. This will be your vitamin to continue treading the path to your dreams.

In this last feature of the V.I.S.I.O.N system, we are going to focus on fear. In one of my favourite books Job says, **'The thing which I greatly feared has come upon me'**. There will be times when your visualisation will take you to your fears like Job. If you intensely visualise your problems, you will become fearful. You will be scared of what you see on the screen of your mind. Do you remember the story I told you from Les Brown about the man who was always afraid of a dog in his neighborhood? This man would always ran whenever the dog until he developed the courage to face the dog. It is only at this point that realized that the dog had no teeth.  Currently, what are you running from?

______________________________________________________

______________________________________________________

______________________________________________________

______________________________________________________

______________________________________________________

______________________________________________________

It is only when we decide to face our fears that we realize like President Franklin D Roosevelt that **'there is nothing to fear but fear itself'**. Some people see FEAR as an acronym for two actions: **F**orget **E**verything **A**nd **R**un and **F**ace **E**verything **A**nd **R**aise. Which action will you take when faced with fear? If I were you, I would **F**ace **E**verything **A**nd **R**aise because I know that the worst thing to fear is fear itself. I would raise and take Dr Norman Vincent Peale's advice to throw my heart over the fence and let my body follow where my heart is. This requires us immense faith. In my favourite book, St Paul says: **'faith is being sure of what we hope for and certain of what we do not see'**. This means that we are sure of what we do not see because of our FAITH: we **F**ind **A**nswers **I**n **T**he **H**eart.

Life is full examples of people who have lived by FAITH in extraordinary ways: Mother Teresa, Nelson Mandela, Martin Luther King Jr, Dietrich Bonhoeffer, and many others. Like is also full of people who have lived by FAITH in ordinary ways: our parents, siblings, neighbours, etc. For example, FAITH is one of the treasures I got from my parents when they walked to their dreams with unresolved determination and hope. This taught me that I can achieve my dreams if lived from a place of FAITH. As you continue to see your VISION, see it with FAITH not FEAR. FAITH with take you to another hemisphere with a different time zone where your dreams are possible.

# Research

Research about one person that has lived from a place of FAITH that you are go to emulate in your life.

_______________________________________________

_______________________________________________

_______________________________________________

_______________________________________________

_______________________________________________

_______________________________________________

_______________________________________________

_______________________________________________

_______________________________________________

_______________________________________________

_______________________________________________

_______________________________________________

_______________________________________________

_______________________________________________

## Do

I want to leave this question with you:  How big is your faith? Your response might be like that of the apostles after listening to Jesus talking about the challenges ahead that caused them to tremble: 'Increase our faith'. This has become my daily affirmation 'Increase my FAITH'. Take time and examine the size of your FAITH.

**Create** *time and space within you*

- ✓ Find a quiet space inside your and outside of you

- ✓ Journey to a special place in your heart

- ✓ Sit down and relax

- ✓ Take time to be you

**Review** *who you are*

- ✓ Start off an inner conversation with yourself

- ✓ Be grateful of who you are today

- ✓ Appreciate who you are: miracle, uncommon, and gift

- ✓ Admire your purpose, your dreams and goals in life

**Reflect** *on your* V.I.S.I.O.N

- ✓ Reflect on your vision

✓ Reflect on your dream

✓ Reflect on your goals

✓ How do I visualise them?

✓ What do I need to change so that I can see my dreams and goals better?

**Visualise** *your* V.I.S.I.O.N

✓ **V**isualise my goals and dreams

✓ **I**nside the mind is the theatre where my goals and dreams are screened

✓ **S**enses are doors to my mind and to my heart

✓ **I**magine my goals and dreams being accomplished

✓ **O**vercome obstacles

✓ **N**o fear is the way forward for me

✓ **A**ppreciate the great and hard work you have done

✓ **N**otice how positive you feel about yourself

**Affirm**

✓ **I** Visualise **Inside** my mind with my **S**enses and I **I**magine **O**vercoming obstacles with **N**o fear.

✓ Increase my F.A.I.T.H

**Take** *action*

- ✓ See with V.I.S.I.O.N

- ✓ Live by F.A.I.T.H

# STEP 6: NETWORK WITH GREAT PEOPLE

'Align yourself with people that you can learn from, people who want more out of life, people who are stretching and searching and seeking some higher ground in life'. Les Brown

# Who is in my network?

When it comes to the people we associate with, there is no shortage of sayings, proverbs and statements. One African proverb says, **'Birds of the same feather flock together'**. Another goes, **'Show me your friends and I will show you who you are'**. Donald Trump says, **'If you hang around with losers you become a loser'. Porter Gale says, 'Your network is your net worth'**. So I say to you if you want be great, surround yourself with great P.E.O.P.L.E© because greatness leaves clues. You might be asking: How do I know who the great P.E.O.P.L.E© are? Here is my simple answer: Great people are P.E.O.P.L.E© who are:

- **P**urposeful
- **E**ncouraging
- **O**pportunity experts
- **P**roductive with their time
- **L**ive full
- **E**xemplary

If you want to be great, take time and apply this formula to the people that you surround with. It is my hope that by the end of this penultimate step, you would have found out who the great people are in your life.

# Acknowledge

Ask yourself, 'Who are the people I associate with?' Make a list of 14 people you associate with. Do not worry if you can't get all the 14 people.

1. ______________________________________________

2. ______________________________________________

3. ______________________________________________

4. ______________________________________________

5. ______________________________________________

6. ______________________________________________

7. ______________________________________________

8. ______________________________________________

9. ______________________________________________

10. ______________________________________________

11. ______________________________________________

12. ______________________________________________

13. ______________________________________________

14. ______________________________________________

Use the following questions to reflect about the people you network with. Be honest with yourself for, if you don't, no one will do this for you.

## Are the people I associate with PURPOSEFUL?

Great people are full of purpose. They know who they are and why they came into this world. You will recognise them when you meet them. They walk with purpose, eat with purpose, drink with purpose, and smile with purpose. They are filled with purpose. Given that they are filled with purpose, their purpose will overflow onto you. Make it your purpose to find people of purpose and get acquainted with them. Ask them what their purpose is and what drives them. Ask them how they walk to their dreams, achieve their goals, and listen to their ideas. Observe their experience with purpose and make them your role models. Who are the purposeful people in my life?

1. _______________________________________________________

2. _______________________________________________________

3. _______________________________________________________

4. _______________________________________________________

5. _______________________________________________________

6. _______________________________________________________

7. _______________________________________________________

# Evaluate

Use these questions to evaluate the relationships you have with these people.

| Question | People in my life |
|---|---|
| Is this a **positive** relationship? | |
| Is this a **negative** relationship? | |
| Do I **smile** when I see this person? | |
| Do I feel **sad** about myself after I been with this person? | |
| Am I **proud** of the things we have done together? | |
| Who should I **count in** when it comes to purposeful people? | |
| Who should I **count out** it comes to purposeful people? | |

# Are the people I associate with ENCOURAGING?

It is necessary that you attract people who are encouraging into your life. Great people are always encouraging you to do what is good. I am reminded of my favourite poem by Mary Stevenson: *Footprints in The Sand.* One of the verse is: '**You promised that if I followed you, you would walk with me always. But I have noticed that during the most trying periods of my life there have only been one set of footprints in the sand. Why, when I needed you most, you have not been there for me? He replied, "The times when you have seen only one set of footprints, is when I carried you"**. As you step into your greatness, it is necessary that you surround yourself with people who lift you up when you fall, people you can learn from because they are the message they bring to you, and people who see the path before you see it for yourself.

1. _______________________________________________

2. _______________________________________________

3. _______________________________________________

4. _______________________________________________

5. _______________________________________________

6. _______________________________________________

7. _______________________________________________

# Evaluate

Use these questions to evaluate the relationships you have with these people.

| Question | People in my life |
| --- | --- |
| Is this an **uplifting** relationship? | |
| Is this a **lowering** relationship? | |
| Does it make me a **better** person? | |
| Does it make me a **bitter** person? | |
| Do I feel that this person will **carry** me in times of trouble? | |
| Do I feel that this person will **abandon** me in times of trouble? | |
| Who should I **count in** when it comes to encouraging people? | |
| Who should I **count out** it comes to encouraging people? | |

## Are the people you associate with OPPORTUNITY experts?

Let me tell you an African folktale. Long time ago, some birds and animals lived in the sky. The dog and the hen lived there, too. One day, it was very cold. The birds asked the dog to go down to the earth and bring some fire to make the sky warm. The dog went to the earth and entered a courtyard near the house. The dog saw many bones, started eating them, and forgot all about the fire. The dog decided to live there. As the birds in the sky were getting colder, they sent the hen. The hen came to the same courtyard. It saw seeds, started eating them, and forgot about the fire. The hen decided to live here. The dog and hen didn't return to the sky as they found better opportunities on earth.

Imagine you are a dog or hen. You have been sent to this amazing earth on a special mission. The earth is your courtyard filled with abundant opportunities. Which people help you see opportunities in your life?

1. __________________________________________________

2. __________________________________________________

3. __________________________________________________

4. __________________________________________________

5. __________________________________________________

6. __________________________________________________

7. __________________________________________________

# Evaluate

Use these questions to evaluate the relationships you have with these people.

| Question | People in my life |
| --- | --- |
| Does this relationship **increase** my opportunities? | |
| Does this relationship **decrease** my opportunities? | |
| Does it make me an opportunity expert? | |
| Does it make me lesser opportunity expert? | |
| Do I feel that this person will **support me** to find better opportunities? | |
| Do I feel that this person will **abandon** me as I search for better opportunities? | |
| Who should I **count in** when it comes to opportunity experts? | |
| Who should I **count out** it comes to opportunity? | |

## Are the people I associate with PRODUCTIVE with their time?

Great people are productive with their time. Great people like Bill Gates and you have 24 hours in a day. Have you ever wondered why people have different levels of success within those 24 hours? To make you wonder even more, some people born many years after you have become more successful than you. What do they do differently? How have you spent you our past years? If you had your life to live again, what would you do differently?

1. ______________________________________________________________

2. ______________________________________________________________

3. ______________________________________________________________

4. ______________________________________________________________

5. ______________________________________________________________

6. ______________________________________________________________

7. ______________________________________________________________

The truth is that there will always be time. The truth is that you and I are running out of time. Our time in this universe is limited. So, use it wisely.

# Evaluate

Use these questions to evaluate the relationships you have with these people.

| Question | People in my life |
| --- | --- |
| Is this relationship helping **manage** my time? | |
| Is this relationship wasting my time? | |
| Does it make me a **punctual** person? | |
| Does it make me a **latecomer?** | |
| Do I feel that this person will **advise** me to use my time wisely? | |
| Do I feel that this person will **mislead** me to waste my time? | |
| Who should I **count in** when it comes to efficient people? | |
| Who should I **count out** it comes to efficient people? | |

# Do the people you associate with LIVE FULL?

Great people live full and die empty. People who live full do not operate in the survival and comfort zones. They refuse to live a life that is below their potential as the greatness within them pushes them to say, **'There is something within me that says I can do better than this'**. They do not settle for less than they are. They refuse to work to survive but work to thrive. They seek to connect with who they are. They use all they are and all they have to live full and die empty.

It is necessary for you to take time and think - if you had your life to live over again, what would you do differently? As you step into your greatness, seek to connect with yourself so that you live to the fullest. Do not live like a happy prisoner who looks through the window of the cell, sees the mud outside and gets scared of coming out. If you are a prisoner, be an unhappy prisoner who sees through the window of the prison cell, sees the stars and is excited to get out and discover more. Stretch yourself beyond your prison and look for the exit to your best life. Remember that there are no limits when you are pursuing your greatness: look at the stars not the mud.

Great people know they cannot help others if they are not living a full life. They have to fill themselves first so that they can share with others from the overflow. Ona Brown says, **'You can't pull out anything out of an empty bag'**. So, drink from people's overflow and fill yourself with greatness. If you continue drinking from people who are empty, you will become empty. They will suck form you all that you have and you will become empty like them. So, find people who are overflowing with greatness.

1. ___________________________________________

2. ___________________________________________

3. ___________________________________________

4. ___________________________________________

5. ___________________________________________

6. ___________________________________________

7. ___________________________________________

**Evaluate**

Use these questions to evaluate the relationships you have with these people.

| Question | People in my life |
| --- | --- |
| Who in my network are is living **full**? | |
| Who in my network is living an **empty** life? | |
| Are they **motivated** from inside? | |
| Are motivated from outside and are being **dragged** in life? | |
| Do they **inspire** me with what they do? | |
| Do they **demotivate** me and I give up what I am doing? | |
| Who should I **count in** when it comes to people who live full? | |
| Who should I **count out** it comes to people who live full? | |

## Are the people you associate with EXEMPLARY?

This is the last feature of great PEOPLE. Great people live as examples. They are the message they bring. So, are the people you associate with good examples for you to follow? When you are going on an unfamiliar journey, it is helpful to go with someone who knows the way. Do the people you associate with know the way to your destination? Are they Satnavs for you to navigate you through all the corners of life to your dreams? Are they your life support system when you run out of oxygen? Are they supportive? Les Brown says supportive and exemplary people are **'not the people you pick along the way. These are people who pick you up along the way'**. As you step into your greatness, be on the lookout for people who pick you along the way, who are seeing things for you, who believe in you and in your greatness. Great people are always there to serve you. They know that you have something special. There is greatness within you. Who are the people you admire? Your role models? Do you have exemplary people in every area of your life? List them and what you admire in them.

1. _______________________________________________________________

2. _______________________________________________________________

3. _______________________________________________________________

4. _______________________________________________________________

5. _______________________________________________________________

6. _______________________________________________________________

7. _______________________________________________________________

**Evaluate**

Use these questions to evaluate the relationships you have with these people.

| Question | People in my life |
| --- | --- |
| Who in my network do I **admire** most? | |
| Who in my network do I **not admire**? | |
| Are they **role models** in what I want to do? | |
| Are they **bad examples** in what I want to do? | |
| Do they **inspire** me with what they do? | |
| Do they **demotivate** me and I give up what I am doing? | |
| Who should I **count in** when it comes to exemplary people? | |
| Who should I **count out** it comes to exemplary people? | |

# Check

Check all your lists and make a promise to end those relationships that are not PEOPLE focused. You have greatness to pursue. Don't let anyone slow you down. In the end, you are responsible for your life. If your life is wasted, you suffer the most and you have only yourself to blame.

## Who should I count in?

1. _______________________________________________

2. _______________________________________________

3. _______________________________________________

4. _______________________________________________

5. _______________________________________________

6. _______________________________________________

7. _______________________________________________

## Who should I count out?

1. _______________________________________________

2. _______________________________________________

3. _______________________________________________

4. _______________________________________________

5. _______________________________________________

6. _______________________________________________

7. _______________________________________________

# Appreciate

You have now reached the penultimate step to greatness. You know that only one step is left to step into greatness. Take time and reflect on the people you associate with. Ask yourself the following questions. What are they bringing into my life? Are they P.E.O.P.L.E©? In other words, are they: Purposeful? Encouraging? Opportunity experts? Productive? Living full? Exemplary? Do they fuel or empty my life? Do they empower me? Do they inspire me to become the best version of me? Do they enlighten my mind and ignite my heart? Choose your top 7 people you are going to go with to the next step. These are the people when you say, **'You promised that if I followed you, you would walk with me always. But I have noticed that during the most trying periods of my life there have only been one set of footprints in the sand. Why, when I needed you most, you have not been there for me? They will reply to you, "The times when you have seen only one set of footprints, is when I carried you"**.

1. _________________________________________

2. _________________________________________

3. _________________________________________

4. _________________________________________

5. _________________________________________

6. _________________________________________

7. _________________________________________

# Remember

Before you go to the final step to greatness, go with PEOPLE and with all that you have learnt about PEOPLE. Climb with the willingness and determination to be a PEOPLE too. Be purposeful with your life. Be encouraging no matter what happens. Be an opportunity expert. Be productive with your time. Live full. Be an example and a message of a great PEOPLE.

# Do

**Create** *time and space within you*

- ✓ Find a quiet space inside your and outside of you
- ✓ Journey to a special place in your heart
- ✓ Sit down and relax
- ✓ Take time to be you

**Review** *who you are*

- ✓ Start off an inner conversation with yourself
- ✓ Be grateful of who you are today
- ✓ Appreciate who you are: miracle, uncommon, and gift
- ✓ Admire your purpose, your dreams and goals in life

**Reflect** *on your network*

- ✓ Who are the people I associate with?
- ✓ Are there great people?

✓ Are there toxic people?

✓ Who do you need to count in or count out?

**Visualise** *the PEOPLE you need in your life*

✓ Visualise your friends, relatives, colleagues, and other people in your life

✓ Ask them the following PEOPLE questions:

✓ Are they purposeful?

✓ Are they encouraging?

✓ Are they opportunity experts?

✓ Are they productive with their time?

✓ Are they living full?

✓ Are they exemplary?

✓ Appreciate the great and hard work you have done

✓ Notice how positive you feel about yourself

## *Affirm*

✓ My life is purposeful

✓ My life is encouraging

✓ I do manage myself not time

✓ I am living full

✓ I want life to use me

## *Take action*

✓ Network with people who are PEOPLE

# STEP 7: TAKE MASSIVE ACTION

**'The path to success is to take determined, massive action'.**

**Tony Robbins**

# Have you ever taken massive action?

Welcome to the last step to your greatness. It is amazing to see how far you have come from. In this final step, we will focus on taking massive action and how that can keep you on the road to greatness. In my eyes, A.C.T.I.O.N© is the difference between success and failure. People are great because they take A.C.T.I.O.N© and make their lives a masterpiece. A.C.T.I.O.N© stands for:

- ✓ **A**sk questions

- ✓ **C**ourageous

- ✓ **T**ake risks

- ✓ **I**nspired by affirmations

- ✓ **O**bsessed with hope

- ✓ **N**ever give up

What actions am I taking to live a great life?

_______________________________________________

_______________________________________________

_______________________________________________

_______________________________________________

_______________________________________________

_______________________________________________

## Ask Questions

Great people ask questions. Like Tony Robbins, great people know that **'successful people ask better questions, and as a result, they get better answers'**. Like the speaker I heard some time back, great people know that **'life is a question and how you live it is the answer'**. So, they decide to live their lives as a question. They ask questions related to their vision because they know that **'where there is no vision people perish'**. They ask: Who am I? Why am I here? What brought me to this planet? What is the purpose of my life? What is my personal mission? How will future generations know that my life was worth living?

## Legacy

Like Les Brown, great people are aware that **'The graveyard is the richest place on earth, because it is there you will find all the hopes and dreams that were never fulfilled, the books that were never written, the songs that were never sung, the inventions that were never shared, the cures that were never discovered; all because someone was too afraid to take that first step, keep with the problem or determined to carry out their dream'**. Great people ask questions related to their personal mission, dreams and goals. Like them, ask - What is the dream for my life? Am I busy living my dreams or dying with my fears? What is it that I want to be my unique contribution to this world? What is my legacy?

_________________________________________________

_________________________________________________

_________________________________________________

_________________________________________________

_________________________________________________

_________________________________________________

_________________________________________________

_________________________________________________

# Imagination

Like Napoleon Hill, great people know that **'what the mind of man can conceive and believe, it can achieve'**. They thus ask questions about the best way to conceive what they want. Like them, study other people and ask - How can I use my imagination? What is the purpose of the movie I am playing on the screen on my mind? How can I put the power of my mind to work? How can I change the movie on the screen on my mind and be successful?

# Network equals net worth

Like Porter Gale, great people know that **'your network is your net worth'**. Like them, review your relationships and ask - Is this relationship purposeful? Is it encouraging? Does it give me the opportunity to meet with experts? Is it a productive use of my time? Is this relationship helping me to live full and die empty? Is it allowing me to have a good example to follow?

## Self-education

Searching for answers to these questions sets them on the road to self-education. Jim Rohn says, **'Formal education will make you a living; self-education will make you a fortune'**. Education is the key to becoming a better and committed builder of your masterpiece. As you know, the world is full of negative information that we feed our minds. For example, when you switch on any news channel, more than half of the news is negative whether suicide rates increasing, war in various countries, stock markets crashing, repossessions, economic depression on the way, crime rates up, deaths, etc. Even our social networking websites are cluttered with poor quality information. When I was growing up, there was only one day when we could be misled - 1st April – April Fool's Day. Today, every day is a fooling day, especially with the explosion of fake news.

Imagine feeding your body with a toxic and poor diet. How will it become? What about not feeding your body at all? What might be the consequences? Just as your body will become malnourished, starved, dehydrated and with the imminent possibility of death, it makes sense that we apply this to our minds too. If you feed your mind with toxic information, it will become toxic. This toxic information will spread and infect your heart as well.

Imagine what will happen to the treasures buried in your heart! What will happen to your miracle power? What will happen to your gifts? What will happen to your greatness? They too will become infected. Now that you have discovered the value of self-education, which 12 books are you going to read this year (only one book per month) to develop yourself?

1. _________________________________

2. _________________________________

3. _________________________________

4. _________________________________

5. _________________________________

6. _________________________________

7. _________________________________

8. _________________________________

9. _________________________________

10. _________________________________

11. _________________________________

12. _________________________________

## Courage

Great people go into action with courage. As you step into your greatness, you will definitely be in battle with your past. It will take you courage to face your past and accept who you are becoming today. It will take you courage to change and become the person you want to be from this day forward. Fortify yourself and know that your courage will come from within you and drive you into action fearlessly. How can you be fearless?

## Take Risks

Great people are risk-takers because they know that they would rather risk and get one percent from life than not risk and get zero percent from life.  They also know that failing to risk is a risk. Like Helen Keller they admit that **'life is a daring adventure or it is nothing at all'**. I am sure you have taken a lot of risks in your life. Even waking up is a risk since you can fall stepping from your bed. Eating is a risk as you might choke. Crossing the road is a risk as you may get run over. Most people are not living their greatness because they do not see beyond the horizons of their problems. Anger, frustration, fear, guilt, unhappiness, and resentment can slow down your steps to greatness. What are your fears?

_______________________________________________

_______________________________________________

_______________________________________________

_______________________________________________

_______________________________________________

_______________________________________________

_______________________________________________

_______________________________________________

_______________________________________________

_______________________________________________

# Overcoming fear

Are you prepared to forever dwell on your fears? I often listen to Les Brown videos. I remember listening to him telling a story of a man who was afraid of a dog in his neighbourhood. Whenever he would pass, the dog would bark and he would run away. One day he decided to face his fear and developed the courage to face the dog. The dog came towards him and he did not run. When the dog reached him, he grabbed it by the collar only to realise it had no teeth. Wow! All those times this man had been running from this dog - it had no teeth! Take courage and face your fears. Like the dog, your fears might not have any teeth. Grab your fears by the collar and show them you are unstoppable. Show them you have miracle power within you. Do not let your fears obscure the steps to your greatness. How are you going to do this today?

# Act

Educate yourself every day because you know knowledge is the new currency. Read daily because you know reading is the food for the mind. Manage yourself better because you know you cannot manage time. Focus on what is going on in the stadium of your mind and not in the football stadium. See what is taking place in the theatre of your heart and not in the world's famous auditoriums. Refuse to be casual about life because you do not want to become a causality. Refuse to be denied by life because you have not given up on life, be unstoppable as you climb the steps to greatness.

# Inspired by Affirmations

Great people use inspiring affirmations which are verbalisations of their inner dialogue. Inner dialogues are likely to happen when the mind and the heart are talking to themselves during meditation, reflection and other moments of serenity.  Some of the affirmations or inner dialogue can be negative and involve self-defeating thoughts. For example, **everything I do never works. Wherever I go problems follow me. I can't do this. This is never going to work for me.** This is negative mind talk. What negative mind talk do you involve in?

______________________________________________

______________________________________________

______________________________________________

______________________________________________

______________________________________________

______________________________________________

______________________________________________

______________________________________________

______________________________________________

______________________________________________

# Positive mind talk

Great people do not entertain negative mind talk. They consciously choose and use inspired affirmations that are positive. What positive things do you say to yourself?

# Affirmations

You might find my collection of positive affirmations below helpful.

- I create what I want in my life.

- I deserve to be happy and fulfilled.

- Every day in every way I'm getting better and better.

- Everything I need is coming to me effortlessly.

- My life is blossoming in total perfection.

- I have everything I need to enjoy my here and now.

- I am the master of my life.

- Everything I need is already within me.

- Perfect wisdom is in my heart.

- I am whole and complete in myself.

- I love and appreciate myself just as I am.

- I accept all my feelings as part of me.

- I love to love and be loved.

- There more I love myself, the more I give to others.

- I now give and receive love freely.

- I am attracting loving relationships into my life.

- My relationship with… is growing happier every day.

- I now have a satisfying and well-paid job.

- I communicate clearly and effectively.

- I have enough time/ energy/ wisdom/ money to accomplish all my desires.

- I am always in the right place at the right time, successfully engaged in the right activity.

- It is ok for me to have everything I want.

- This is an abundant universe and there's plenty for all of us.

- Abundance is my natural state of being.

- Every day I am growing more financially prosperous.

- The more I have, the more I have to give.

- The more I give, the more I receive, the happier I feel.

- It's ok for me to have fun and enjoy myself, and I do!

- I am relaxed and centred.

- I have plenty of time for everything.

- I am now enjoying everything I do.

- I feel happy just being alive.

- I am healthy and beautiful.

- I am open to receive the blessings of this universe.

- I have a wonderful job with wonderful pay.

- I offer a wonderful service in a wonderful way.

- The greatness within me is creating miracles in my life.

- All things are now working together for good in my life.

- I am now attuned to my higher purpose in life.

- I now recognise, accept, and follow the divine plan of my life as it is revealed to me step by step.

- I give thanks now for my life of health, happiness, and self-expression.

- I can do everything with Christ who strengthens me.

- My God is guiding me in everything that I do.

- God lives within me and manifests in the world through me.

- The light of God surrounds me, the love of God enfolds me, the power of God flows through me. Wherever I am, God is, and all is well.

Remember, you can do affirmations silently or verbally, write them down, sing them, or do whatever works for you. Affirmations need to be phrased positively and in the present. This acknowledges that they have already happened in your mind and what is left is making them happen materially.

## Obsessed With Hope

One of the biggest challenges facing our world today is the shortage of hope. I remember being told a story about a town in Europe. Whereas people in the western part of this town were affluent, those in the east were poor. Whereas people in the western part of this town lived longer, those in the east had shorter lives. The main reasons people in the western part were affluent and lived longer was because they had unlimited hope. They were obsessed with hope. The main reason people in the eastern part were poor and lived shorter lives was because they had a shortage of hope. They were hopeless.

As you step into your greatness and inspire others to do so, remember that people are failing to reach their greatness not because of the place they are born, not because of their career and not because of their gender or race. The main reason people are failing is because of the size of their hope. While some people are unwilling to hope, others completely refuse to hope. My question to you is - what is the size of your hope? Are you ready to measure the size of your hope? Are you willing to increase the size of your hope to greatness? What are you willing to do or change after reading this book so that you increase your hope? I leave you with the words I heard from Pope Francis in February 2017, **'Hope does not disappoint. Hope is sure. Be men and women of hope'.** If you want to be great, increase the size of your hope. This will allow you never give up.

## Never Give Up

Say: **'I've had it...I've had it'**. In life there are going to be moments when you going to say to yourself and to others, 'I've had it'. There are the moments when you know that whatever you are doing is not in line with your purpose and is derailing you from your dreams and goals. These are the moments when you know that if you continue doing, staying, studying or working where you are, you are destroying yourself. These are the times where you are not going to tolerate injustice in your life. These are the moments when you are going to leave the old you and walk towards the new you.

In these moments, taking A.C.T.I.O.N© will mean letting your fears go. In these moments, you need to call upon the hope within you and resolve to never give up. In times like these, never giving up will mean that you are determined to reset the clock and look for answers to your new life elsewhere. Once the universe notices your determination and relentlessness to never give up, it will allow you to step into your greatness.

Let me leave you with the story of the builder that I heard from a famous speaker. It touched me and I remember it whenever I am in a situation that requires me to not give up:

> *There was a man who was an efficient builder. He had worked for years in a large company for many years and reached the age of retirement. His employer asked him to build one more house. It was to be his last commission. The builder took the job but his heart was not*

*involved. He used inferior materials. Timber was poor. He failed to see them many things that should have been clear to him had he shown normal interest in his work. When the house was eventually finished his employer came to him and said the house was yours. Here is the key. The builder immediately regretted that he had used the worst materials and engaged the most incapable of workers. If only he had known that the house was for him.*

If the builder had made a commitment with his life to not give up until his last day on the job, if he had made a resolute decision that he was going to give it his best, he would have appreciated the gift.

As you step into your greatness, do not be like the builder who gave up on the last day. Become a no matter what person. When you are a no matter what person, you set high standards for yourself all the time. When people hear your story and see you as someone who never gives up, they should be able to say **'Because of you I am not giving up. Because of you, I am alive today. Because of you, I am stepping into my greatness'.** This is my story and I am stepping into my greatness.

# LIVE YOUR GREATNESS

'I believe in you. I believe in your dreams. Live as a masterpiece because you are a piece of the master'.  Dr Patrick Businge

Congratulations you have completed the *7 Steps to Greatness*. What a journey you have had in climbing these steps. Now, let us look back and see what has happened on your journey and how you have grown.

On the first step, you had the chance to search and find yourself. You now know that you are a miracle in manifestation. You are uncommon and unrepeatable. You are a gift gifted with greatness. With this self-knowledge, your life has taken on a new meaning and your eyes were now opened to see a new horizon. But you did not stop there. You went on to take the second step.

In the second step, you took time to discover your purpose in this immense universe. You searched within yourself and found what you desired most. You found your why for living. You are now guarding what you have found like the apple of your eye. But you did not stop there. You took the next step.

In the third step, you allowed your purpose to give birth to your wildest dreams. You took James Dean's advice and were able to 'dream as if you will live forever'. Dreaming while you were awake allowed you to discover your earliest dreams. Your dreams were big dreams because you knew from James Allen that dreamers were the saviours of the world. Your big dreams made you step out of your comfort zone and now you have been able to witness defining moments unfold in your life. But you did not stop there. You took the next step.

In the fourth step to greatness, you learnt a unique set of goals – **S.T.A.R**©️ goals. You felt them strongly in your heart and connected them to your dreams. And as they occurred in the theatre of your mind, you were able to visualise them. While they became absolutely necessary to you, they have become a life and death issue too. You also set goals that were ridiculously hard to achieve because like Dr Norman Vincent Peale, you knew you were shooting for the moon and not the stars. This is because you became aware that when you begin stepping into your greatness, the process is more important than the outcome. But you did not stop there. You took the next step.

In the fifth step, you were able to see your dreams and your goals. You used your **V.I.S.I.O.N**© to go into another hemisphere with a different time zone, where your contemplated your dreams. You **V**isualised **I**nside your mind with your **S**enses and **I**magined **O**vercoming obstacles with **N**o fear. This system allowed you - inside your mind - to have what you wanted. You realised that it was better to live from your imagination and not your memory. You overcame obstacles because you were now living from a place of FAITH and not of FEAR. You created a vision-board where you displayed your vision, your dreams and goals. But you did not stop there. You walked to the penultimate step.

In the sixth step, you contemplated what Porter Gale said that 'your network is your net worth'. You thus dedicated your time to reviewing your network using the **P.E.O.P.L.E**© model. You asked questions about the people you associated with: What were they bringing into my life? Were they purposeful? Encouraging? Opportunity experts? Productive? Living full? Exemplary? You went deeper and asked more questions: Did they fuel or empty my life? Did they inspire me to become the best version of me? Did they inspire my mind and ignite my heart? Did they empower me? What was I becoming emotionally, academically, financially, and spiritually because of these people?

Upon asking and answering these questions, you offloaded toxic people and uploaded great people into your life. But you did not stop here. You made the commitment and kissed the final step.

In the seventh and final step to greatness, you made an unwavering decision to take massive action. You refused to park your dreams on the motorway of life. You committed to following the incredible **A.C.T.I.O.N**© system to make this happen. Using this system, you emulated great people and asked important questions about your life, your dreams, goals and vision. You left no question unanswered and embarked on the road to educate yourself because you knew education was food for the mind. You knew the value of feeding your mind with good quality self-education and were, more than ever, committed to doing whatever it took to have what you wanted.

Now that you have reached the last step, you do not have to stop moving. It is time for you to even double your speed as you cruise on the motorway to your greatness. There are no more steps for you. You are now very special. You are a miracle child. You are uncommon. You are gifted with greatness. You are in this universe for a purpose. You have lots of dreams within you. You have the power to use **S.T.A.R**© goals and live your dreams. Step into action now. Walk with faith and show the world that you are unstoppable. Manifest your gifts and demonstrate to your community that you are an asset and not a liability to them. Live full and die empty. I believe in you. I believe in your dreams. Go and live your life as a masterpiece because you are a piece of the master.

# ABOUT THE AUTHOR

Born in a small village in Uganda, Dr Patrick Businge did not let his circumstances characterised by war and abject poverty become his standard. Following his dreams while believing that no condition was permanent, he took steps to raise above his circumstances and made greatness his benchmark.

Dr Patrick Businge has gone on to become the Founder of Greatness University: the world's first institution dedicated to discovering, unlocking, and monetising greatness in individuals and businesses. His main goal is to help you tap into your greatness faster and easily than you can ever imagine.

Dr Patrick Businge is an educator. He has taught over 50 000 people in classrooms, churches, orphanages, villages, community centres, and boardrooms throughout the United Kingdom of Great Britain, Europe, Africa, and the Americas.

Dr Patrick Businge is also a strong believer in lifelong learning and personal development. He has studied in over 7 universities and acquired over 10 postgraduate qualifications. He has researched, written and spoken for approximately 20 years in the fields of ethics, philosophy, religion, education, armed conflict, disability, and greatness. Living in a world characterised by war, plagued by a shortage of hope and marred with average performance, his ultimate vision is to inspire one million people become instruments of peace, messengers of hope and channels of greatness.

Dr Patrick Businge speaks to various audiences on Personal and Professional Development. His exciting talks, transformational seminars and life changing boot camps on *7 Steps to Greatness*, Book Writing, Self-Esteem, STAR Goals, Success Mindset, and Finding Your Best Self bring about immediate change and long-term results.

Dr Patrick Businge has travelled and worked in over 10 countries on 3 continents. He speaks four languages: English, French, Swahili and some Arabic. Patrick is happily married and has 2 children. He is active in community and national affairs. To learn more about his programs, seminars and services, please visit www.greatness-university.com. If you have any personal questions email him directly at info@greatness-university.com or meet him on Facebook, Twitter, LinkedIn and Instagram.

# BY THE AUTHOR

*7 Steps to Greatness*: The **Masterplan** to Take Your Life, Studies, Career and Business to the Next Level

*7 Steps to Greatness*: The **Workbook** to Take Your Life, Studies, Career and Business to the Next Level

*7 Steps to Greatness*: The **Journal** to Take Your Life, Studies, Career and Business to the Next Level

*7 Steps to Greatness*: The **Seminar** to Take Your Life, Studies, Career and Business to the Next Level

*7 Steps to Publish the Book in You:* The **Retreat** to Discover, Write, Publish and Monetise your Book

**Greatness University:** Online courses at www.greatness-university.com

Author contact: info@greatness-university.com

# 7 STEPS TO GREATNESS SEMINARS

Most people are not living their dreams because they are living their fears. In this foundational training, you will deepen your awareness of the 7 steps that will take fear out of the process and turn your dreams into reality. You will learn the core strategies Dr Patrick Businge has learnt from his mentors like the world's number one motivational speaker Les Brown and has used in his path to greatness. These strategies will help you to live your dreams and cruise on the path to your greatness.

When you complete this course, you will:

- Discover the greatness within you

- Develop your mindset for greatness

- Create a formula on finding your purpose

- Design a three dimensional lifestyle

- Develop and use STAR goals

- Deliver your success like all great people.

You have something special. There is greatness within you. Everything you need to live a great life is within you. This training will give you strategies to access your greatness, inspire confidence in your mind, and ignite your heart to go after your dreams.

# BOOK WRITING RETREATS

A lot of people want or have at least thought about writing a book. This is because there are a lot of benefits to having a book with your name on it. Writing a book and becoming a published author allows you to position yourself as an expert in your field, increase your credibility, share your message with the world and transform your business. However, few people ever write and publish their book. When you come to our retreat, you will discover that writing your book is not that complicated. We will give you a 7 step roadmap to write, publish and monitise your book. In this roadmap, you will get the strategies that we have acquired from our mentor: Brian Tracy, bestselling author of over 83 books, on how to:

- Discover the book within you

- Learn the blueprint to write and design your book

- Learn and develop the skills to become a great author

- Publish and promote your book

- Turn your book into a profitable business.

You have something special. There is a book within you. Come to our book writing retreats and discover, write, publish and monetise the book within you. Allow the world to read and be transformed by your message.

Greatness University was born out of the realisation that we live in world where we are sold almost anything and everything except one important product: greatness. So, we decided to become the world's first institution dedicated to discovering, unlocking, and monetising greatness.

We believe greatness leaves clues. We are therefore committed to helping people like you tap into their greatness faster and easily than you can ever imagine. We do this by researching greatness in individuals, organizations, businesses, and other spheres of life. We help people like you create their own personal economies by monetising their greatness. We guide people like you on the best ways to create a lasting legacy. Remember, your legacy is not what you give to the people you love but what you will live in them.

At Greatness University, we partner with like-minded people to unlock greatness around the world. We offer online courses, run face to face training, give one to one mentoring, and organize boot camps in our areas of expertise worldwide. Our courses and mentoring in the Principles of Greatness, Setting STAR Goals, Live Your Dreams, Walk in Greatness, The Millionaire in You, Speak and Change the World, and Discover the Book in You are not only focused on developing your mind but also speaking to your heart: where your treasure is.

As world leaders, our faculty members are always learning. They are mentored by top experts and great people in the world like Brian Tracy, Les Brown, Omar Periu, and Ona Brown. You have something special. There is greatness within you. Allow us to help you tap into your greatness faster than you can ever imagine so that you may make your life a masterpiece. To discover more about our work, visit us at www.greatness-university.com. We look forward to working with you and walking the path to greatness together.

PATRICK BUSINGE
'This first moving book is full of great ideas that will inspire and motivate you to achieve all your goals'.
- Brian Tracy, Bestselling Author.
7 STEPS TO GREATNESS
BEST
amazon.com
SELLER

# The Road To Your
# BEST SELF

## Discover the Miracle Power, Uncommon Nature and Greatness in You

## DR PATRICK BUSINGE